MICHIGAN STORIES FOR NEWCOMERS

Andrew's Journey to a New Life in America

Barbara Vaille and

Jennifer QuinnWilliams

Illustrations by Barbara Goodsitt

THE UNIVERSITY OF MICHIGAN PRESS

Ann Arbor

Published in the United States of America
The University of Michigan Press
Manufactured in the United States of America
⊗ Printed on acid-free paper

2010 2009 2008 2007 4 3 2 1

ISBN-10: 0-472-03233-X
ISBN-13: 978-0-472-03233-4

To the Reader:

This book was written for your pleasure. It is written in simple English for adult English language learners. We hope you will enjoy the story and learn English at the same time. When a character is speaking in Chinese, the speech appears in *italics*. When a character is speaking in English, the type does not change. Andrew's English is not always perfect, of course, but it is written for authenticity of someone at his language level.

Happy Reading,
Barbara and Jennifer

Dedicated to all of our classroom volunteers over the years.

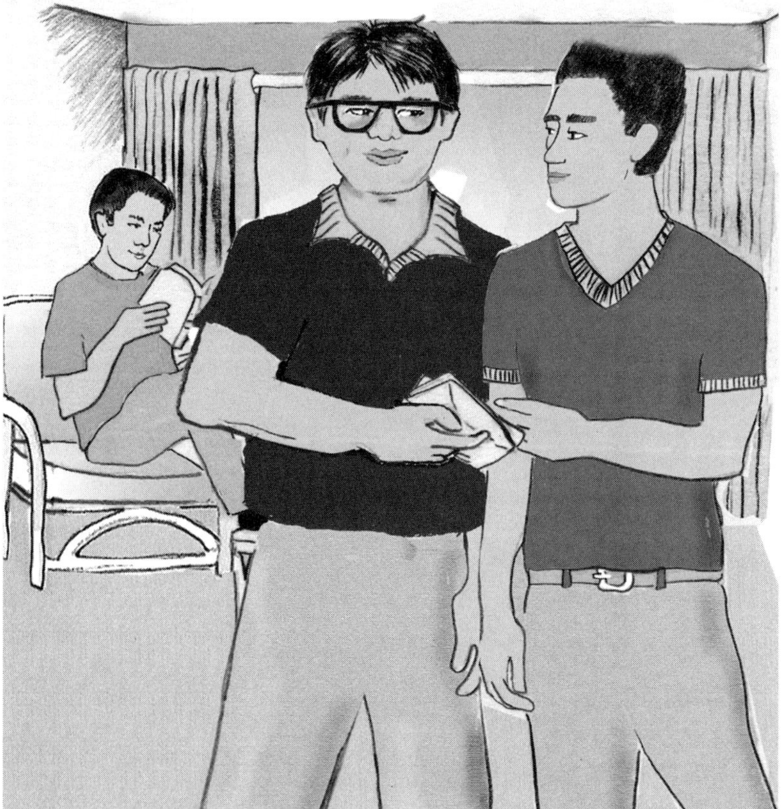

CHAPTER 1

"*Order up!*" shouted the cook. He tossed the plates of sesame chicken and shrimp with garlic onto the order table and went back to his cooking. Andrew grabbed them and rushed through the kitchen door into the restaurant. He served the dishes to his table and rushed back just in time to hear the cook shout again, "*Order up!*"

"Busy tonight," Andrew said to no one. He was practicing his English, even though he almost never got a chance to use it at work because everyone spoke Chinese. The waiters who spoke better English than Andrew took the orders from the customers. Then, Andrew served the dishes, filled the water glasses, and cleared the tables.

Andrew ran back and forth all night from the kitchen to the tables. When the restaurant closed, he ate a quick meal and cleaned up the dining room. He set the tables for the next day. Finally, he told Jimmy, the owner, that he was going home. He got his coat and walked back to his apartment. He shared the apartment with two other Chinese men. One man, Charley, worked at the restaurant with him. The other man, Wei, had a very good job as a computer programmer.

Wei and Charley were sitting in the living room when Andrew got home. Wei was watching TV, and Charley was reading a book.

"Charley, do you want to go to English class with me tomorrow?" Andrew asked.

"That's just a waste of time," said Wei. *"You only go once a week. How can you learn anything?"*

"I'm going to go more often," said Andrew. *"There's a class on Thursday mornings from 8 to 10."*

"How can you go from 8 to 10? You start work at 10."

"The teacher told me I can leave at 9:30."

Wei waved his hand in the air. *"You won't learn anything. It's a waste of time."*

Charley looked up from the book he was reading. *"Don't listen to Wei,"* he said. *"Go to the English class and study when you can. That's what I do."* He held up his mystery novel. *"When I finish this book, I'll go back to the library and get another. Jimmy promised me that I'll be the next waiter because my English is improving so much. Thanks for inviting me to class, but I have to be at work early tomorrow to help Jimmy with the new menu."*

Andrew nodded. He wanted to believe that Jimmy would keep his promises to them. He remembered meeting Jimmy, the owner of the Chinese restaurant, in Hong Kong. Andrew's boss in Hong Kong knew that Andrew was moving to the United States so he introduced Andrew to Jimmy.

He knew that Jimmy liked to hire Chinese employees. Jimmy said that Americans liked to see Chinese people working in a Chinese restaurant. Jimmy promised Andrew that if he signed a contract with him, he would give him a very good job in the U.S. with good wages.

"You'll start at the bottom and learn everything," Jimmy said. *"As soon as you learn English, you'll be a waiter and make a lot of money."*

"I'm a good cook, too," Andrew told Jimmy. *"I work in one of the best restaurants in Hong Kong."*

Andrew's job in the restaurant in Denver was not what was promised, though. Night after night, he served the orders and cleaned up. He never learned anything else from Jimmy. When he complained, Jimmy said his English wasn't good enough.

"How can I learn?" Andrew asked. *"I only have one day off."*

Jimmy shrugged his shoulders. *"Everyone has problems. You have to work harder."*

Andrew knew that if he had time, he could learn more English. Once he learned better English, maybe he could go to a community college or even a university. From there, who knew? He could do anything!

"I really hope you get the waiter job," he told Charley. *"I used to think that's what I wanted, too. Now, I'm not so sure. My contract with Jimmy is for one more year. Then, maybe I will find another job*

with more time off. I want to learn good English as soon as possible."

Charley grinned. *"I know what I want. More money!"*

Andrew and Wei laughed. Wei handed Andrew some envelopes. *"You got some mail,"* he said. *"Looks like a bill and something else!"* He waved a light blue envelope in the air. *"This one is addressed to Li Yingen. Who uses your Chinese name?"*

Andrew smiled. "*Just give me the mail,*" he said. Wei knew the letter was from Andrew's fiancée in Hong Kong. She always used his Chinese name. She didn't like his English name.

Wei grinned and gave him his mail. Andrew put the letter from his fiancée aside. He would save it for last. He opened the first bill. It was his credit card statement. The total was $450.35.

"What is this?" he exclaimed. This couldn't be his bill. "*I only used my credit card one time, at the grocery store!*"

Andrew was careful about his charges. He looked at the name on the statement: Andrew Lee. He took his credit card out of his wallet and checked the account number on the statement to make sure it matched the number on his card. It did.

He looked at the charge. It was from a Marley's store. He never went there. It was too expensive for him.

"What's the matter?" asked Charley.

"Look at this bill! It says I owe more than $450. I didn't buy anything from Marley's."

"Did someone steal your credit card?" asked Charley.

"No, it's right here." Andrew showed him his card.

"Let me see the bill and your card," said Wei.

Andrew handed them to him. Wei looked at them carefully.

"There's an 800 number on the bill," he said. *"That's a phone number you can call to ask questions or make complaints. Call it, and tell them you never made the charge."*

Andrew took the bill and looked at the phone number. He felt very nervous. What if he called and the person who answered didn't understand his English? What if he or she didn't believe him? What if the person believed him but said he had to pay anyway?

"What should I say?" he asked Wei.

"Say: There is a problem with my credit statement. *Then, when they ask you what the problem is, you say:* I was billed for a charge I didn't make."

Andrew repeated the phrases. Then he dialed the 800 number. The phone rang. An automated voice came on the line. He understood the first sentence, which was, "Thank you for calling Visa card customer service." But then, the voice started speaking in Spanish. It paused and began again in English. The only word he understood then was "please." He hung up.

"It's too hard," he said. *"It's not even a real person!"*

"As soon as you hear a voice, try pressing zero," said Wei. *"That sometimes gets you an operator or a customer representative."*

Andrew nodded. He swallowed hard and dialed the number again. This time, he pressed zero as soon as the voice came on the line. Another voice, a woman's voice, said, "All of our customer representatives are currently busy. Please stay on the line...." He hung up again.

"I'll go to the credit card office in the morning," he said. *"It's easier to explain in person."*

Wei sighed. *"There's no office to go to. Do you want me to call for you?"*

Andrew felt embarrassed. He wanted Wei's help because $450 was a lot of money, but this was his problem. *"No, no, I'll do it. I can go to my bank,"* he said.

"I insist," said Wei.

"Thank you," said Andrew. He handed Wei the credit card and the bill. Soon Wei was talking to someone from the credit card company. He spoke so fast that Andrew only understood a word or two. Someday, Andrew promised himself, I will speak English like that. Then, I can solve my own problems.

Wei hung up and said, "*You only have to pay*

$50 of the bill, but you have to send in some forms to tell them what happened. And the company cancelled your card. You'll get another one in the mail. The person I talked to said that you might have a bigger problem, though."

"Why did he say that?"

"Well, since your card wasn't stolen, the person who used it to charge on your account must have the card number and some personal information about you. The thief probably made the charges over the telephone or maybe even online. He may be using your identity for other things, too."

Andrew was shocked. *"What kind of other things?"*

"To open new accounts or borrow money," said Wei. *"The customer representative said you should order your credit report."*

Andrew shook his head. *"I don't know anything about all that."*

"This is serious," said Wei. *"You should take care of this as soon as possible."*

Charley spoke up. *"Andrew, Jimmy always says that he'll help us with any problems. This is the time to ask him for help."*

Andrew didn't like to ask Jimmy for help. Jimmy never did anything for anyone without it costing something. Andrew didn't have money, but Jimmy might ask him to work extra hours, wash his car every day for a month, or help paint one of the buildings he owned. He wouldn't help Andrew for free.

"I'll talk to him tomorrow," said Andrew.

After thanking Wei, he went to his bedroom. He was tired and confused. It was late, but he decided to read the letter from YaoLin, his fiancée, before he went to bed. He opened the envelope and unfolded the letter. There was a photograph of YaoLin inside. He looked at it and began to feel better. She was so pretty. She was looking over her shoulder at the camera. She was smiling, and her thick, black hair was cut in a new, modern style. It fell to her shoulders in layers. He began to read.

Dear Yingen,

With this letter I send my sincere wishes that you are well and happy. Thank you for your last email. I wish you had a computer. It's nice of your roommate to let you use his sometimes, but I would like to email you more often. When we are married, this won't be a problem. We'll talk to each other every day.

I'm sending you this picture so that you will recognize me when you pick me up at the airport. Are you surprised at that? I have very good news. Remember, in your last letter you asked me to come to Colorado and visit you? My answer is yes! I am so happy and excited. My parents were worried about me traveling alone at first. But, I found a ticket that takes me to Denver with only two stops. I will arrive in Denver at 3:06 PM on January 21. That's just a week before Chinese New Year! We can celebrate together for the first time in two years.

Love,

YaoLin

Andrew felt his cheeks flush. This was good news. YaoLin was coming to visit in a few weeks. He looked at her photograph again. She was wearing a red blouse and tight jeans. He noticed how slim and attractive she was. He remembered their dates in Hong Kong. They liked to take the bus to "The Peak" at the top of the island and look out over Victoria Bay. They liked to dance at the discos or go to karaoke with their friends. They liked to stay up late talking about their future together. He remembered when they decided to get married. They were afraid to tell their parents because they were so young. But their parents were very happy. The two families were friendly, and everyone approved the match.

Then Andrew won the diversity lottery. The lottery allowed him to emigrate to the United States. He felt like the luckiest man in Hong Kong. He and YaoLin decided to wait to get married until he was settled in the U.S. *"When you are prosperous, you'll come back to Hong Kong, and we'll get married. Then, I'll move to Colorado with you,"* said YaoLin. Andrew smiled at the memories.

He read the rest of her letter and carefully folded it. He opened the drawer in his nightstand where he kept YaoLin's other letters and put the new one inside. He laid the photo on the nightstand.

"I talk to Jimmy tomorrow," he said out loud. He liked to practice his English by speaking out loud when he was alone in his room. With YaoLin's picture beside him, he almost felt like he was talking to her. "He help me with credit card. I ask him give me time off. I plan great visit for you, YaoLin."

CHAPTER 2

The alarm clock beside Andrew's bed buzzed loudly. He groaned, reached over, and pressed the off button. The silence was a relief. Andrew looked at the time: 6:00. He told himself he could stay in bed ten more minutes. He was dreaming about YaoLin.

They were walking hand-in-hand in the rose garden in Denver's City Park by the Nature and Science Museum. The flowers were in full bloom, so beautiful and fragrant. The view of the city skyscrapers and the mountains beyond was clear and...suddenly Andrew opened his eyes and looked at the clock. Oh, no! It was 6:48.

Andrew threw back his covers and got up. He headed to the bathroom to take a quick shower. Wei was already gone, and Charley's door was closed. He was still sleeping.

Andrew had tea and rice soup for breakfast. He zipped up his coat and put on a hat and gloves. He heard on the radio that the temperature was 41 degrees and breezy, with a high expected of 49. It was cold but mild for January. The sun was shining as it did most days. Denver was a nice place to live. Andrew thought of YaoLin. He said to himself in English, "She like sun. I hope she like Denver, too. I wait only two and one-half week. Then she arrive."

He left the apartment to make the 20-minute walk to the big, old school where the English class was. He hoped to have enough time to write about his credit card problem in his journal before class started. Writing in a journal was always their homework. The teacher, Karen, called it "standing homework." She wrote a journal prompt on the board as an idea for the students to respond to. But they could write about anything.

The thought of writing reminded Andrew that he needed to email YaoLin tonight. Using Wei's computer was okay, but YaoLin was right. It would be better when they were married and talked to each other every day.

Andrew's thoughts turned to his credit card problem. He was worried about the charges, but he didn't want to ask Jimmy for help. Maybe Charley was right. It would be okay to have Jimmy check his credit report.

When he entered the class, Karen, the English teacher, greeted him. "Hi, Andrew. This is a surprise, to see you in the morning class. Did your work schedule change?"

"No," replied Andrew. "But I want learn more English. I leave 9:30. Remember?"

"Oh, that's right. We talked about this before the Christmas holiday. Class starts in about ten

minutes. I'll introduce you when the other students come. Linda and I are discussing today's lesson."

Andrew turned to look at the young woman standing beside Karen. She was slim and taller than Karen. She had long, straight auburn hair. A beautiful red, orange, yellow, and green scarf was draped around her shoulders. She smiled and stepped up to Andrew to shake his hand.

"Hello. My name is Linda. What's your name?"

"Andrew Lee. Nice to meet you. Are you teacher?"

"No. Actually, I'm an artist. But I help in the morning class on Thursdays. My friend Flor told me about the school, and I decided to volunteer."

"Oh, is good help to Karen," said Andrew. He looked at her face. She was looking at him with big brown eyes. "Excuse me. Now I write journal," he said.

"Okay," said Linda. "Maybe we'll have a chance to talk later, and I can get to know you."

"Okay," answered Andrew as he sat down to write.

The lessons in January were about health. Today, the focus was on stress. As a whole class they talked about things that were stressful in their lives. Andrew spoke about working long hours and sometimes being too tired to attend class. He didn't share his news about his fiancée coming or the credit card situation with the other students.

Then, in small groups, the students discussed

what to do about stress. Karen and Linda sat with individual students and read and responded to their journals. Karen sat with Andrew. She read:

> January 5
>
> Today I have big problem. Yesterday I get letter from credit card company. They say I spend $450. But I not go this store. I not spend money. Maybe is too big problem. Maybe someone have my number and use my name. Do you have idea for me?

"Oh, Andrew. How awful! What did you do when you got the letter?" asked Karen.

"I try to call on phone—800 number. So difficult in English with machine voice. Wei, my roommate, call for me. They tell him maybe the people has my credit card number and know about me. I have the card. They not have the card. Now I get new card. I scare about this."

Karen wrote in Andrew's journal:

> This is a serious problem. If someone stole your name, that's called identity theft. I just read an article about it in the newspaper last week. I think it's still in my recycle bin. I'll get it and bring it to class for you."

"Thank you, Karen," Andrew said after he read Karen's response.

"Do you have any questions about what I wrote?" asked Karen.

"I no make mistakes?" wondered Andrew.

"Yes, there are some grammar mistakes. But I understood everything you wrote, and that is enough for today."

Andrew said, "Okay. Now I go work."

After saying goodbye to Linda and the students, Andrew left.

Work was busy from the moment Andrew arrived. Finally, after lunch, he had a chance to go to Jimmy's office. He knocked on the door. His boss was sitting at his desk filling out some forms. The desk was covered with piles of paper. Andrew knew from his experience in restaurants in Hong Kong that the owners and managers were always busy ordering supplies and doing payroll. But he never saw anyone with as much paperwork as Jimmy.

"Excuse me, Jimmy. I'm sorry to interrupt you. I have a problem."

"I'm busy. Is it important?"

"I'm sorry. Yes. It is about my credit card," answered Andrew.

"Come in," said Jimmy in a nicer voice as he moved the stacks of paper to the other side of the desk. *"What is it?"*

In the back of his mind, Andrew thought that Jimmy suddenly was being very polite. He wasn't speaking quickly, as if he was too busy, like he usually did. Andrew sat down. He told Jimmy the whole story of the credit card problem. He said he was worried about identity theft. Jimmy listened sympathetically.

"Charley suggested that I ask you to call about my credit rating. Since you are my employer, you must know about that," said Andrew.

"Sure, I can order your credit report. It will tell me your rating and what loans you have. If anyone is using your name, your credit report will show loans you didn't take out. Don't worry. I'll see what I can find out and let you know."

"Thank you, Jimmy. Thank you very much."

"You are welcome. You are a hard worker."

As he left, Andrew thought, *if I'm such a hard worker, when is he going to make me a waiter? My English is good enough for that.* Something else was strange: Jimmy was very agreeable, just like he was in Hong Kong when Andrew first met him. He didn't ask Andrew to do anything in exchange for checking his credit rating. Was that a good omen? Maybe Jimmy really did appreciate him.

Andrew went into the kitchen to help the cook prepare for the dinner crowd. Jimmy stuck his head in the door.

"Hey, Andrew, I have to go out. I won't be back in time to lock up. You do it for me, okay?"

"Okay," said Andrew. *"I'll take the keys from the nail by the back door."*

"Good," said Jimmy.

Charley and Andrew both worked the dinner shift. The work was steady but not as busy as lunch or weekend dinners. When they were both at the beverage station, Charley asked Andrew if he had talked to Jimmy.

"Yes," answered Andrew. *"He said he will check my credit for me."*

"Great. See? Jimmy's not a bad guy. He said he would help you, and he will," said Charley. Andrew was glad he had to take tea to some customers. He didn't want to tell Charley his negative thoughts and questions about Jimmy.

Andrew didn't hear anything from Jimmy until the next week. Then Jimmy called him into his office. "*Andrew, I checked your credit report, and it's all fine. I put a copy in your personnel file. There are no late payments or unusual transactions. Let me know if you have other questions or problems with this.*"

"That's a relief. Thank you for your help, Jimmy."

"I'm glad to do it," said Jimmy.

Wei was watching TV when Andrew and Charley came home that evening. "Hey, man," he said in English. *"You're looking happy, Andrew. Not tired and depressed like I expected after working all day and with the mess with your credit card."*

"Yes. I have good news. Jimmy said my credit is fine. No problems. Jimmy was nice. I think he will

give me some time off when YaoLin comes to visit on January 21st. I am making plans to show her around Denver, take her to my English class, and go to the mountains. Maybe we will try skiing," said Andrew.

"Oh, keeping secrets, eh? Why didn't you tell us last week when her letter came? Where is she going to stay?" asked Wei.

Andrew's face grew pink. *"She will stay here, in my room. I'll sleep on the couch."*

"Ahhh," said Wei with a wink and a sly smile.

After a minute, Wei continued. *"The mail came. A letter for Charley and three things for you."* He handed the envelopes to the two men.

The top envelope on Andrew's pile said Visa Card Services in the return address. *"This must be my new Visa card,"* he said as he opened the envelope. Sure enough, it was a shiny new Visa credit card with his name on the front.

He read the information with the card. He understood that he needed to sign the back of the card right away, so he did. The information said the card was not yet activated, but it was easy to do by calling a toll-free number. Andrew swallowed. He didn't want to talk on the phone in English again. But he had to try.

Bravely, he dialed the number. He heard an automated voice. Andrew listened carefully. He followed the voice's directions and entered the new card number. The voice said, "Your card is now activated and ready to use. Thank you for choosing

Visa." Andrew let out a breath. Then he took out his wallet and put the new credit card away.

He looked at the two other envelopes. He didn't recognize the return names or addresses. He opened the first one. It was a form letter. "Dear Friend of Public Radio," it began. Andrew scanned down the page. At the bottom was a section to tear off. There were little boxes beside amounts of money. His name and address were printed there, too.

"What's this?" he asked Wei and Charley.

Charley shrugged his shoulders. *"I don't know,"* he said.

"Let me see," said Wei. *"Oh, it's just junk mail. Americans are always sending out stuff to get money. Just throw it away."*

Andrew felt uneasy. He didn't like having his name and address printed on that form. He put it aside for the moment and opened the third envelope.

It was a bill from a home improvement store. It said, "Payment due February 8: $284.16."

"What? What is this? Again?" he cried. He gave the bill to Wei.

Wei looked at it and then looked at Andrew. *"This isn't good. You're in trouble."*

CHAPTER 3

"I'll call the company right now," said Andrew.

"Do you want me to do it?" asked Wei.

"No, this time I'll do it myself. I'll press 0 to try to talk to a real person, and I'll ask him to speak slowly."

Wei nodded. Andrew made the phone call. But when the automated voice came on, it told him to call during normal business hours between 8:00 AM and 5:00 PM. He was so frustrated that he wanted to slam down the phone, but what good would that do? He hung up.

"I'll have to wait until the morning," he said.

"A few more hours aren't going to make much difference," said Wei.

Andrew sat down on the couch next to Wei. *"What are you watching?"*

"I'm watching a show called 'Friends.' A woman at work told me it's very funny. But I don't know what's so funny about it."

Charley sat down, too. The characters on the show were looking for something in someone's apartment. They talked a lot and made funny faces.

"Do you understand what they're saying?" asked Charley.

Wei and Andrew answered at the same time. *"Yeah,"* said Wei. *"A little,"* said Andrew.

"Well, I prefer to read." Charley went into his room.

Andrew stood up, too. *"Good night,"* he said to Wei. Wei nodded at him. But he didn't take his eyes off of the television screen.

Andrew tossed and turned in bed. He couldn't sleep. He wanted to fix this problem of someone buying things by using his name. He wanted to talk to YaoLin and make sure all the arrangements for her trip to Denver were confirmed. He also wondered if Jimmy really checked his credit report when he said he did. Jimmy had no reason to lie to him, did he?

Andrew sat up and turned on the light. He got out his cell phone. He looked at it, and then at his watch. It was 1:00 AM on Wednesday morning in Denver. That meant it was 4:00 PM Wednesday afternoon in Hong Kong. YaoLin usually got home from work at 3:30. He took his calling card out of his wallet and dialed her number.

YaoLin picked it up on the first ring.

"YaoLin! It's me, Yingen!" he said. *"How are you? What are you doing?"*

"Yingen, I'm so happy to hear your voice," said YaoLin. *"What a lovely surprise!"*

Andrew laughed happily. He decided not to tell YaoLin about his credit card problem. Instead, he asked her about her day and their friends. They talked and talked. Finally, he asked her about the trip.

"I'm so excited!" she said. *"The days don't pass quickly enough."*

It made Andrew feel very good to hear that. They talked about the airport and where Andrew would wait for her, and then YaoLin asked about Denver's weather.

"It's very nice here," said Andrew. *"It's almost always sunny. But remember, it snows sometimes, and it's usually cold. Bring some warm clothes."*

"I've never seen real snow," said YaoLin.

"You'll like it. It sparkles in the sunshine."

After another minute or two, Andrew realized his calling card minutes were almost gone. He and YaoLin said goodbye and hung up. Andrew lay back down on his bed with a smile on his face.

In the morning Andrew called the home improvement store. He had a long conversation with a customer service representative. Several times he asked the representative to speak slowly, and he asked a lot of questions to make sure he understood what the representative said. Finally, he understood. This problem could not be fixed over the phone. He would have to go to the store with his identification card and fill out a special form that said that he didn't buy the item charged to him. The company was going to cancel the account right away, but the representative said, "The sooner you get to the store, the better."

Andrew called Jimmy to tell him he might be late to work. Jimmy was not happy. *"What am I supposed to do with all the customers who want their glasses refilled and their plates served?"* he demanded.

"I'm sorry. Jimmy, this is the same problem you helped me with yesterday. I was charged for things I didn't buy."

Jimmy was silent for a minute. *"Just don't make this a habit,"* he said.

When Andrew got to the home improvement store, he found the customer service desk and showed the clerk his bill. He tried to tell her his problem, but she was not as nice as the phone representative. She was impatient with him.

"I charge for thing I not buy," he told her. He pointed at the bill. "This thing I not buy."

She looked at the bill. She blew a bubble with her chewing gun. "You Andrew Lee?"

"Yes."

"This your address?" she asked.

"Yes."

"You got a receipt?"

"No, I not buy this. I not open account."

Finally, she asked him for his identification card, handed him some paperwork, and went to make a copy of the card. He looked at the forms he had to fill out. They looked long and complicated.

When the representative came back with his card, he asked, "Can I take papers home?"

"I guess so," she said. "Be sure to bring them back, though. We'll have to process them and try to see who opened the account."

Andrew felt like she was accusing him of trying to cheat the company. He was very embarrassed, but what could he do? He tried not to show his embarrassment, confusion, and anger.

"Thank you. I bring . . . I will bring forms back."

He wanted to take the forms to Karen. She always seemed to be glad to help the students with anything. He would ask her for help during journal time. But it was already 9:15, and he had to be at work at 10:00. If he took the bus to school and then walked to work, he would be late. Maybe he should ask Jimmy to help him. Andrew sighed. Jimmy was such an unpleasant guy. Andrew didn't know what to do.

Finally, he rode the bus to school. Karen was teaching the class, but Linda, the new volunteer, was sitting close to the door. Andrew waved at her to come outside the classroom. She did.

"Is something wrong?" she asked.

"Oh, no," said Andrew, smiling. "I just need little help with papers." He held out the forms. "You help me?"

Linda took the forms and read the instructions. "Did someone steal your charge card for this store?" she asked.

"No. I never have card. Maybe identity theft."

"Oh! Sure, I can help you with this. Let's go to

the teacher's lounge where we can have some privacy."

Andrew liked that. She understood how embarrassing this was. They went into the teacher's lounge, and Linda quietly helped him with the forms. When they were done, she asked, "Are you going to take these papers back right now?"

"No. I want take, but I not have time today. I have to go work."

"I think it's pretty important that the papers get back to the home improvement store right away. Do you have a car?"

"No. I take bus. Not worry. I will take tomorrow morning."

"How about if I drive you to the store, then to work? You're already late; it won't take all that much longer if I drive you."

Linda spoke in a deep, slow voice that sounded like music to Andrew. She was easy to understand, even though she used some phrases and words he didn't know. He liked her.

"Thank you, Linda," he said. "But I have to go work. Too much trouble you."

"No trouble! Really, I'd like to do it."

"Really?"

"Really."

❖

As they drove to the home improvement store, he and Linda talked. She was easy to talk to. When they got to the store, she waited in the car while he took the papers in. Then, she drove him to work. Even with her help, he was still 45 minutes late. He thanked her and rushed into the restaurant.

Jimmy was standing by the door waiting for customers.

"Finally," he snapped. *"And who was that? I thought you said you were taking care of a problem. That girl didn't look like a problem to me."*

Andrew didn't like the tone of Jimmy's voice. *"She works at the school where I take English classes. She gave me a ride so I could be here sooner. She's a nice woman."*

"Sure, sure," said Jimmy. *"Now, get to work."*

Andrew worked hard all day and all evening. Jimmy was mad at him, so it didn't seem like there was ever a good time to tell him that he wanted some time off to spend with YaoLin. Finally all the customers left. Jimmy was in his office, counting out the money from the day. Andrew went in to talk to him.

"Jimmy, I'm sorry I was late today," said Andrew. *"It was the first time in two years."*

Jimmy nodded and put the money in a bank deposit bag. He looked at Andrew. *"Is there something else?"*

"Yes. My fiancée is coming to visit me. She's coming on January 21. I want to take some time off."

Jimmy smiled. *"I remember your fiancée. A very pretty girl. You can have one day off."*

"I planned to take a couple of days off. Is it possible?" Andrew asked. Jimmy picked up the bank bag and stood up. *"No. You can have one day off. Just don't think you can have Chinese New Year off. Pick some other day."*

Andrew didn't know what to say. One day? After two years of work and no extra days off? And he did want Chinese New Year's day off. He remembered what YaoLin wrote in her letter: We can celebrate together.

Jimmy was already walking out the door. *"Come on, you don't want to sleep in here, do you?"*

Andrew followed him out. Charley was waiting for him outside, and they walked home together. He told Charley about Jimmy. *"What will I do? YaoLin will expect me to spend a lot of time with her, not just one day a week. I thought Jimmy might give me a week off."*

"Did you tell him that?"

"No. Do you think I'm crazy? I don't want to lose my job."

"You always think Jimmy is such a bad guy. I think if you talk to him and explain, he'll give you more time."

Andrew didn't want to disagree, so he said, "*Yes, maybe you're right.*"

He and Charley walked the rest of the way home in silence.

On January 21^{st,} Andrew stood in the airport terminal outside the secured area, waiting for YaoLin. They saw each other at the same time.

"Yingen!"

"YaoLin!"

Smiling, he rushed to her and took her bag. He kissed her cheek and she blushed. She tucked her arm into his. Andrew suddenly felt shy. He and YaoLin used to know each other so well, but that was two years ago. Now he was a different man. She was a different woman.

"I'm happy to be here, but I'm so tired," said YaoLin. *"I was too excited to sleep on the first airplane, and then I rushed to get through customs and catch the second airplane. I want to sleep for a week."*

Andrew thought about making a joke. He could say something like, *"Lucky for you, I won't have any time off, so you can sleep until you go back to Hong Kong!"* But that didn't seem wise. Instead he said, *"My friend Wei gave me a ride to pick you up. He's waiting for us. We'll have a nice, quiet ride into Denver, and then you can rest."*

Andrew saw Wei waiting for them. He introduced YaoLin to Wei and then collected her bags while Wei went to get the car. As they left the terminal, YaoLin gasped.

"What's wrong? Are you alright?" asked Andrew.

"It's so cold!"

YaoLin was wearing Capri jeans and a cute

embroidered jean jacket. Her shoes were fashionable blue high-heeled pumps. She looked beautiful, but she wasn't dressed for the cold. Andrew took off his warm down jacket. He put it around YaoLin's slim shoulders.

"Where's your coat?" he asked.

"I have a raincoat in my suitcase."

Andrew didn't think a raincoat was going to be warm enough for Denver's winter. He didn't say anything about it, though. Instead, he helped her into the car and put her bags in the trunk.

On the drive from Denver's airport into the city, Andrew tried to see the scenery through YaoLin's eyes. The wide, grassy plains spread out beside the highway. They seemed endless. Far away, the snow-capped Rocky Mountains looked like giant paper cones framed against a deep blue sky. In front of the mountains, the high-rise buildings of downtown Denver looked like shiny metal boxes. Andrew was very happy that the sun was shining and that the view of the mountains was clear. Sometimes they were covered by clouds or hidden by pollution, but not today.

"What do you think?" he asked YaoLin, turning to her in the seat beside him.

He was surprised to see that she had tears in her eyes.

"What happened here?" she asked.

"What do you mean?"

"Why is everything dead? The grass is all

brown. Where are the trees? What happened here? It's terrible."

From the front seat, Wei started to giggle. *"It's winter,"* he chuckled.

YaoLin gave Andrew a questioning look.

"You know about winter," he said, smiling. *"Everything is sleeping. It will all turn green in the spring."*

"Oh, how stupid!" sighed YaoLin, rubbing her eyes. *"I thought...I thought it would be all covered with snow. I didn't think about everything being asleep. It's just so, so . . . brown."*

Andrew gently touched her cheek. *"You're tired. Look at the mountains. They're covered with snow. The snow doesn't last very long in Denver, though."*

YaoLin was very quiet for the rest of the ride. When they got to the apartment, Andrew asked her if she was hungry.

"I think I will feel better if I just go to bed and sleep," she said. *"I'll eat tomorrow."*

Andrew showed her his room. For the first time since the car ride, she smiled, showing a dimple in her smooth, pale cheek. *"Where are you sleeping?"*

"On the couch," he said, blushing.

She put her arms around him, and he kissed her.

The next morning, Andrew's alarm clock rang at 8:30. He quickly shut it off and got up. He showered and dressed in the bathroom, then sat on the edge of YaoLin's bed.

"YaoLin," he whispered. *"I have to go to work. I'll be back at about 10 tonight. Maybe 9:30."*

YaoLin opened her eyes. *"9:30? Tonight? You'll be gone all day and all evening?"*

"Yes. Yesterday was my day off. I have to work today. But Wei will be home at 5:00, and he will take you out to dinner."

"Oh."

"I'm sorry, YaoLin. I left a present for you on the kitchen table."

YaoLin sat up. *"I have a present for you, too,"* she said.

"You can give it to me tonight," said Andrew.

At work, all he thought about was YaoLin. He called home at noon and talked to her for a few minutes. She said she was watching TV and reading and just waiting for Wei to come and take her to dinner. She sounded bored.

Finally, at 9:15, Jimmy locked up the restaurant. Andrew walked quickly in the direction of the apartment.

"Hey! Why are you in such a hurry?" said Charley. He was running to keep up with Andrew.

"You know why!" said Andrew.

Charley laughed.

When they got home, Wei and YaoLin were sitting in the living room. They were both dressed in nice clothes. YaoLin seemed much happier. She stood up and said, *"Wei found a karaoke bar! We're going out to sing karaoke."*

"Right now?" asked Andrew. *"I just got home. It's late."*

"It's not too late for karaoke," said YaoLin. *"Come on, change your clothes. Please?"*

Andrew couldn't resist the look on YaoLin's face. She loved karaoke. She loved to listen to the singers as they read the lyrics and tried to perform like their favorite stars. She loved to perform. She especially liked to do duets with Andrew.

He went into his room and changed into clean jeans and a loose, white long-sleeved shirt. YaoLin smiled at him when he returned to the living room.

"Now we can have some fun," she said.

But YaoLin didn't like the karaoke place they went to. She didn't know the songs they were singing. There was a contest that night, so she didn't get to perform. The next night, Andrew took her dancing. She didn't like it, either. It was too crowded, and she thought everyone was drinking too much.

"Yingen," she said on the third day, *"Don't go to work today. Let's go shopping. I'm bored all day by myself. I'm spending more time with Wei than with you!"*

Andrew sighed. He was very tired from staying out late two nights in a row. He wanted to go to work and then come home and sleep.

He sat down next to YaoLin on the couch. *"I can't stay home today. It's Friday, one of the busiest nights at the restaurant."*

"But I need a warm coat. It's so cold here. If I had a warm coat and a good hat, then I could take some walks during the day. Now, I'm too cold to leave the apartment."

"I'm taking Monday off, and then Tuesday is my day off. Soon, we'll have two days together. We can shop and go sightseeing."

YaoLin was looking at Andrew strangely. *"Do you only have Monday and Tuesday off?"*

"Yes. I told you that."

"But I thought you had Sunday off, too. Sunday is Chinese New Year," YaoLin said quietly. Andrew heard the disappointment in her voice. He felt terrible. But he also felt so tired. Didn't YaoLin understand how hard he was working? He was working for YaoLin, for himself, for them. When he finished his contract, he would have money saved. Then, he would get a better education and a good job, and he and YaoLin could have a good life together. He told YaoLin all of this.

"I know," she said. *"I'm sorry. I just thought it would be different. I thought we would have a good time, like we did in Hong Kong. Do you remember how we used to take long walks and talk and talk?"*

Charley and Wei were gone, so Andrew reached out and took YaoLin's hand. He leaned over and kissed her.

"Someday it can be like that again," he said. But he wondered if that was true. He wanted so much from this new life in America. It seemed that YaoLin wanted the old life in Hong Kong.

CHAPTER 4

The next evening, before Andrew came home from work, YaoLin sat quietly on the couch. She was thinking. She wanted to believe Andrew. She wanted to believe that someday they would be together and happy like they were two years ago in Hong Kong. They were once so close, like best friends. Then they told each other everything and shared happy times. Things were different now.

She looked at Andrew as he came in the door. He was more serious. He always looked tired and worried, not carefree like in Hong Kong when he was a chef in a restaurant. Then people complimented him all the time on his cooking. She remembered that he used to like to make dinner for her and their friends on his days off. Did he ever cook anymore, she wondered? What did he do for fun? Why didn't Jimmy treat him with more respect?

YaoLin had all these questions in her head, but she was uncomfortable talking to Andrew about them. They were walking on eggshells around each other. Andrew sat down beside her. She laid her head on his shoulder. Tears came to her eyes.

"What's the matter, YaoLin?" asked Andrew. *"Don't cry. Everything will work out."*

"I'm not sure," sighed YaoLin. *"Things have changed between us. I don't know this new, Americanized Andrew. I miss Yingen."*

"It's late, and we're both tired. Let's go to bed. I'll give you one of my heavy sweaters tomorrow, or maybe you can borrow a coat from Charley. He's more your size. On Monday we'll go shopping for warm clothes for you. I'm disappointed not to have Sunday off for New Year, too. I wanted to show you how much fun we can have in Denver. But the restaurant will be really busy all day long. I'll ask Jimmy if I can have a few hours off. That's better than nothing."

"Okay," said YaoLin, yawning.

On his way to work on Sunday, Andrew thought about the day before. Jimmy was in such a bad mood that Andrew didn't even ask him if he could have part of New Year off. He didn't have the heart to admit this to YaoLin. She was already disappointed with winter in Denver and his schedule. He didn't want to add to her disappointment. Andrew wondered if that was also why he hadn't told her about the identity theft problem. He asked Wei not to mention it to her, either. But, in a way, it was driving him and YaoLin apart. He didn't like having secrets. He wanted to share everything with his fiancée. If they didn't talk now, while they were engaged, what would their marriage be like?

Work was frantic from the moment Andrew arrived. The restaurant was very clean and neat. Cheerful Chinese characters hung from the ceiling. Bright posters with "Prosperity" and "Good Luck" written in red in Chinese calligraphy and decorated with fancy designs hung on the walls.

At lunch time, every table was taken. People stood in the foyer waiting to be seated. Waiters took orders quickly but politely. Cooks swiftly chopped and stir-fried and then called, *"Order up."* Busboys quietly and speedily helped the waiters carry out the meals, filled water glasses, cleared the dirty dishes away, and reset the tables for the next customers.

During a lull in activity, Andrew looked up from filling a water pitcher to see Wei and YaoLin being led by Jimmy to a table nearby. Andrew smiled. He took the water pitcher to their table.

"This is a surprise!"

"YaoLin said she wanted to see where you work and what keeps you so busy that you can't spend more time with her," Wei said in a teasing voice.

Andrew looked at YaoLin. Her cheeks were pink from the cold. She looked pretty and petite, wrapped up in his heavy green sweater. She was smiling.

"We just saw the Lion Dance at the Far East Center. It wasn't like Hong Kong. It was a very small celebration. It was fun, but now I'm hungry. What is good here?"

"Of course we have dim sum for New Year. The head cook is really good. I'll make sure everything is special for you and tell your waiter," said Andrew. He looked over and saw Jimmy watching him.

"I'll be back in a minute," he said as he went to the next table to fill water glasses. Then he hurried into the kitchen.

"My girlfriend from Hong Kong and my roommate are at table 3. What's the best dim sum tonight?" Andrew asked the cook.

"Don't worry. I'll make sure they get the best in the house." The two men talked for a few more seconds about what YaoLin would like, and then Andrew told their waiter.

Andrew only had a few minutes here and there to talk to YaoLin and Wei. Finally, after they had green tea and fortune cookies, they got up to leave. They waved to Charley across the room and told Andrew they would see him back at the apartment after work.

YaoLin was alone watching TV, but she turned it off when Andrew came home. Her eyes were red from crying. Andrew gave her a hug and a kiss and sat down beside her. She handed him a small slip of paper.

"This was in my fortune cookie," she said. Andrew read, "Your future and true happiness lie across the ocean."

"Andrew, I think it tells the truth. I am not happy here. We have both changed. I will always love you,

but now our paths are different. I think about this all the time. I don't want to wait here in your apartment every day for you to come home. You are working hard, but you should be cooking, not busing tables. When will this change? Wei is nice, but I came to be with you. It is too cold here for me. The best thing now is to change my airline flight and go back to Hong Kong. I want to go back home."

Andrew was silent. In his mind he knew that YaoLin was right. But his heart was heavy and sad.

"I think about this also. But I don't want to leave the United States. Things are not perfect here, but there are opportunities and exciting challenges. I'm looking toward the future."

The two talked late into the night, not quite ready to let go. Then they agreed. They called the airlines and changed YaoLin's ticket to Tuesday. That gave them all day Monday to spend together. There was no need to buy a new winter coat now.

On Thursday in his English class, Andrew sat quietly, hardly participating. During small group time, Karen and Linda sat with individual students to read their journals. Linda sat beside Andrew. "Are you okay? You seem so quiet," she said.

"Is all here in journal," answered Andrew.

February 1

My fiancée go back to Hong Kong before yesterday. We decide no get married. She not like winter. She boring here. Too difficult. I not have time off to be together. Now I worry. I not do anything about identity theft for one week. I have trouble.

Linda responded:

I am so sorry to hear that your fiancée went back to Hong Kong and that you will not marry. I know how excited you were that she was coming to visit. I remember talking about places to go so she would not be bored. It is difficult to have a long-distance relationship. It is so easy to grow apart when you are not in the same place.

English class is not a good time to discuss your identity theft situation. You have my phone number. Please call if you have questions, need help, or just want to talk to someone. You can call me at night after work. I often stay up late and paint.

"Look at the phrases that I underlined. Compare them with your journal entry. If you don't understand, ask me or Karen," Linda said.

Several days later, Wei was working at his computer in his bedroom when Andrew came home from work. He called Andrew in to look at what he was working on.

"Hey, Andrew. Look at this. I was just messing around on the computer, looking up stuff on the Internet, and I found this on Identity Theft and Identity Brokers. Someone probably sold your identity to the people who used it. There's also information about an ID Theft Affidavit. Did you fill out one?"

"No. What is it?"

"It's some papers you use to report information so that you aren't responsible for any debt or charges that someone else made using your name."

"I filled out papers at the home improvement store. Is that the same?" asked Andrew.

"I don't know. Here, I'll print it, and you can see. It looks like there are some other things you have to do."

"But everything is okay at the bank. I closed the account and got a new credit card. And I haven't received any bills from other stores."

Wei handed the papers to Andrew. *"Somewhere I read that you're still in danger. You have false hope because they didn't take your card, just the number. But you don't know what they found out about you with that number. They probably know all about you—your social security number, your address, everything. Maybe they opened up a bank account somewhere else, or got another credit card in your name and are charging things at lots of stores."*

"What should I do?" asked Andrew.

"Read those papers. I'm going out now, but I'll try to help you when I get back," Wei answered as he put on his coat.

Andrew started to read. There was a lot he didn't understand. He was tired, worried, and alone. He needed someone to talk to, someone to help him. Linda. He looked at his watch: 10:20. It was late, but she said she stayed up late. He got out her number and dialed.

"Hello?"

"Hello, Linda? Is Andrew. I call not too late?"

"Oh, hi, Andrew. No, this is fine. I finished what I was painting. I'm cleaning up now, so it's okay. How are you doing?"

"I not know. Wei, my roommate, is give the papers about identity theft. He get the computer. Is difficult. I no understand."

"Your roommate got some information off the Internet for you? Okay. Do you know the website? Never mind. Wait a second. I'll get on my computer and see what I can find. Don't hang up. I'll be right back."

Soon Linda was looking at the same papers that Andrew had. "Listen," she said. "I want to take a closer look at this. Let's get together on your day off. We can go out for coffee and talk after your class. Be sure to call me if you get any phone calls or more mail about this before then." They made plans about where to meet and hung up.

When Andrew arrived at the coffee shop, he saw Linda and walked over to her. She was wearing a pretty blue and green scarf and sitting at a table with Flor from the English class. She greeted him warmly. Flor stood up.

"Stay, stay!" said Andrew.

"I go work now. Sorry, no stay," answered Flor. She said something to Linda in Spanish, which made her laugh. "Bye," said Flor.

She left and Andrew sat down. "You speak Spanish?" Andrew asked.

"Yes," said Linda. "My father was from Mexico."

"Really?"

"Really," said Linda. "Let's get to work."

She handed him a list of things for him to do. He needed to contact one of the nationwide consumer reporting companies to place a fraud alert on his credit report.

"There are three companies: Equifax, TransUnion, and Experion. You have to get a copy of the report from each one."

"Oh, Jimmy got copy of my report," said Andrew.

"Find out which company he got it from. You can contact the other two."

"Okay."

Andrew also needed to notify the police to file a report and fill out the ID Theft Affidavit. She showed him the numbers to call. They practiced a phone conversation. Then they agreed to meet the next week.

❖

All during February and into March, Linda and Andrew met weekly at the coffee shop. He showed her the two credit reports he ordered after talking to Jimmy. They had requests from two banks and one credit card company. "Isn't this strange? Jimmy must have a much earlier version of your report," Linda commented. Andrew received bills from three stores showing large purchases. Linda gave him the confidence to fill out the reports and make the necessary phone calls.

Sometimes they talked at night. Work was the same. Jimmy was the same. Andrew missed YaoLin and wasn't sure they made the right decision. He still had identity theft problems. But on the nights when he talked to Linda, Andrew went to sleep thinking about her and her colorful scarves, pretty auburn hair, and wide smile.

One Thursday morning in class, Flor said to Linda in Spanish, "Linda, what's going on? You never help me with my journal anymore. You're always helping Andrew. I saw you together at the coffee shop again. You look different from when we worked together at Burger King. I think your life agrees with you."

Several other Spanish speakers nodded or smiled and made kissing noises. Andrew watched as Linda's cheeks turned pink. He didn't know what they were saying, but he guessed it was about the two of them since he heard them say his name. He opened his notebook and pretended to read.

CHAPTER 5

Andrew and Linda were sitting in the coffee shop near the school. Andrew felt a little nervous. He practiced what he wanted to say in his mind.

Then he said, "Linda, thank you for all your help with this identity theft problem."

Linda smiled at him. The smile made him blush because it was so friendly.

"I like being with you," she said.

"Oh! Me, too," said Andrew. He paused. Then he said quickly, "I want do something special say thank you. I want make for you special dinner. Do you come my apartment tonight for dinner?"

Linda laughed in surprise. Andrew was embarrassed. He thought asking her to dinner was a mistake. He laughed, too. Maybe she would think it was a joke.

Then Linda said, "I would really like that. What time do you want me to be there?"

That afternoon, Andrew shopped. He didn't have time to go to the big Asian market in the suburbs of Denver. He didn't even have time to go to the stores on Federal Boulevard, which were closer to his house. He went to the local supermarket down the street and bought the freshest vegetables, chicken, and shrimp he could find. Then he went back to his apartment.

He cut up the chicken and shelled the shrimp. He was slicing the vegetables when Wei came home.

"Hey, what's all this food for?" asked Wei. *"Did you get a raise? Did Jimmy finally make you a waiter? Are we celebrating? You should have called me to tell me. I'm going out with some guys from work tonight."*

Andrew grinned. *"It's not for you."*

Wei raised his eyebrows. *"Not for me? Who's it for, then? Not Charley. He's at work. Are you going to eat all of this yourself?"*

Andrew got the wok out of the cupboard. *"My friend is coming over at 7:00."*

"Friend, eh? What kind of friend?"

"Just a friend."

Wei stole a carrot from the cutting board. *"This is pretty good food for a friend.* Girlfriend?" He said the last word in English.

Andrew laughed and threw a chunk of cabbage at Wei. *"Mind your own business. Just be out of here by 7:00!"*

Wei picked up the cabbage and threw it back. *"I don't think I'll leave until 7:05. I have to see this mystery person."*

The two men laughed, and Andrew told Wei a little about Linda.

"She is a big help to me, and I want to do something nice for her," he said.

"That's all? You're just returning a favor?"

Andrew shrugged, and Wei laughed again. Soon, he left to join his buddies. Andrew looked at the telephone. Wei got a lot of phone calls, and Andrew and Charley sometimes got them, too. He didn't want anyone to call while Linda was there. He didn't want to be interrupted. He unplugged the phone.

At 7:00 the doorbell rang. Andrew greeted Linda, and they went into the kitchen. She gave him a bottle of sparkling cider. "Do you drink?" she asked.

"Of course," said Andrew. It seemed like a silly question.

"I mean, do you drink alcohol," said Linda with a smile.

"Oh, sorry! Not too much. But only on special time."

"Well, don't worry, this is cider. It's non-alcoholic."

"Thank you. We drink after dinner." He put the cider in the refrigerator. "Everything ready now. Are you hungry? I make a lot."

"Yes, I'm hungry!" said Linda. "I love to eat. Tell me about the food. Is it all Chinese?"

As Andrew served Linda, he explained each dish. He described how to make them and told her where he learned how to make them. "Put some rice in bowl," he said, "Not too much! Rice make you too much full. Now you try this one. My mother learn me how make this one. Don't mix up the food kind. One at a time."

Linda and Andrew ate and talked. Andrew taught her the Chinese names of the food they were eating. They laughed together at her pronunciation. She told Andrew about her art. She told about how she was an assistant manager at Burger King for a long time, because she didn't think being an artist was a serious profession and she needed to make money. Then one day, she realized she wasn't happy doing that. She enrolled in art school. She explained that she didn't have a choice about doing art, she just had to.

"Do you know that poem by Pablo Neruda that starts, 'And it was at that early age...Poetry arrived in search of me'?" asked Linda.

Andrew really didn't understand what Linda said, but he just answered, "No."

"Well, never mind. I didn't look for art, it looked for me. Do you know what I mean?"

"Maybe," said Andrew. He was enjoying just looking at Linda and hearing her voice. He didn't understand every word, but he knew she was telling him how important art was to her.

Linda smiled and looked down at her bowl. "Oh, look. It's empty." She held it up. "Let me help you clean up."

Andrew put some music on, and they put the dishes in the dishwasher. Then he opened the cider and they went into the living room to drink it and listen to the music.

"I love this song," said Linda.

Andrew stood up. "Do you dance with me?" he asked.

Linda looked surprised, and for just one moment, Andrew felt shy. But then, she held out her hand and said, "Yes."

The next day, Andrew felt like he was walking on air. He was so happy. He thought about Linda, about dancing in his living room, and about the kiss they shared before she went home.

All that changed when he walked into the restaurant.

"Where were you?" yelled Jimmy the moment he saw him.

Andrew was confused. He looked behind him. Jimmy couldn't be talking to him. He wasn't late. There was no one else there.

"I was at home," he said.

"I called you and called you yesterday. I needed you to work. And I needed you to be here early this morning. You never answered the phone!"

"I was gone most of the day," said Andrew. He didn't tell Jimmy about unplugging the telephone.

"I need employees I can depend on," grumbled

Jimmy. *"Not some lazy fool who can't even answer his own phone."*

"Sorry, Jimmy," said Andrew. *"Why did you need me on my day off?"*

"We got a big catering order. You go help prep. Then, you and Charley can help me take it."

"Today is Charley's day off," said Andrew.

"No, I told him to be here at 11:30."

Jimmy stomped away, grumbling to himself. Andrew went into the kitchen and helped the cook prepare the dishes for the catering job. The cook's mood was as bad as Jimmy's.

"It's always an emergency with Jimmy. He didn't tell me about this until yesterday when I saw the order form on his desk. But he knew about it three days ago. Why didn't he tell me? I had to shop for special ingredients this morning. This is crazy." The cook shoved some spices and sauces at Andrew. *"You know how to make this. Get it ready while I go outside and have a smoke. Jimmy isn't going to ruin my whole day."*

"You're a good cook," said Andrew. *"You have your residence card. Why do you keep working here?"*

The cook laughed, but he was not happy. *"I'm no fool. Jimmy doesn't let you go until he wants to get rid of you for his own reasons. I want to stay on his good side, not get hurt."* He sounded bitter.

"What do you mean?"

"Never mind," said the cook. *"I've said too*

much." He put down his knife and went out the back door to smoke.

Andrew began to work. He enjoyed making food, so he tried to forget the cook's strange words and focus on preparing the sauce. Soon he ran out of soy sauce. Jimmy stored cases of things in the back of his office, so Andrew went into Jimmy's office to get another bottle of soy sauce.

As he walked by Jimmy's desk he knocked some files onto the floor. Quickly, Andrew bent down and picked them up. He saw his name on one. He looked up to see if Jimmy was coming. No one was around, so he opened the file. There was his employment application, with his social security number circled in red. Also in the file were some tax forms and a few small photos of him. There was no credit report. Andrew was confused. Jimmy told him he put the credit report in Andrew's personnel file. Why wasn't it there? And why did Jimmy have pictures of Andrew?

Andrew closed the file and put it back on the desk. Jimmy told him his credit report was fine, but there was no report. Why was Jimmy lying to him?

Andrew took a bottle of soy sauce from an open case and went back to the kitchen. He needed to think, but he didn't have time during the day. He and the cook made food for 40 people, and then he and Charley and Jimmy delivered it. He wanted to accuse Jimmy of lying to him, but Charley was in the car, and then they were back at the restaurant getting ready for the dinner rush. Jimmy left early. He told Andrew to lock up.

After the last customer left, Andrew went back to Jimmy's office. He wanted to see the file one more time. He wanted to be sure Jimmy lied to him. But he couldn't find the file. It wasn't on the desk anymore. And now the file cabinet was locked. He opened Jimmy's desk and took out a long, sharp letter opener. He thought he could open the filing cabinet with it. Suddenly, he heard Jimmy's voice from the dining room. He was yelling at Charley for leaving the vacuum cleaner in the middle of the floor. Quickly, he dropped the letter opener back in the drawer and hurried into the kitchen. When Jimmy came in, he was sweeping the floor.

"You two should be gone by now. You're too slow. I should hire some better workers, not such lazy bums. Get out of here. I have work to do." Jimmy went into his office and slammed the door.

Andrew shook his head. Jimmy was usually a little mean and impolite, but never this mean and impolite. Something must be wrong, thought Andrew. Something must be very wrong.

❖

With Linda's help, Andrew got his identity theft problems solved. For several weeks, he didn't receive any new bills or any reports of new accounts opened. He was happy about that, but Jimmy's lie bothered him.

Finally, even though he didn't have the proof that Jimmy was lying, he told Linda about it.

They were walking in Washington Park. It was a beautiful day. The sun was shining, and the sky was a special, clear blue you often see in Colorado. There were many people all around, riding bikes, jogging, and pushing strollers. Linda enjoyed poetry, and she was teaching Andrew a love poem.

"I don't understand," laughed Andrew. "Poetry is too hard!"

"Listen with your heart."

"My heart don't have ears."

Linda smiled and put her hand in his. "But your heart definitely knows about love, doesn't it?"

Andrew didn't answer. He just squeezed her hand. She made him so happy, but he wondered if you could love someone who didn't speak your language. Could you love someone from a different culture? He needed to think about it. He changed the subject.

"I don't tell you before, but I think Jimmy lie to me that he got my credit report." He told her there was no report in his file in Jimmy's office.

"Andrew! That's terrible. Jimmy really isn't a very nice guy, is he?"

"No. Not at all."

"I wonder why he didn't tell you the truth." Linda was quiet for a moment. Then she said, "Andrew, you have to confront him. You have to go in there and ask him why he lied to you."

"I think about it, but I don't have truth."

"You mean proof."

"Yes, proof. And Jimmy my boss. I careful what I say him."

"It doesn't matter!" said Linda, with excitement. "You should demand to see your personnel file. And if you're right, then you should ask why he lied. There's something really strange about all of this. Jimmy knows everything about you, doesn't he? When you were born, what your social security number is. I bet he even knows your parents' names, doesn't he?"

"More. He know my parents. He meet them in Hong Kong."

"Oh, wow. I'm getting a bad feeling, Andrew."

"Me, too," said Andrew miserably. He was getting a bad feeling for two reasons. One was, he thought Jimmy might be involved in his identity theft. The other was Linda's suggestions. Andrew wasn't the kind of person to rush in and confront someone angrily. He liked things to remain friendly. Jimmy wouldn't just say, *"Oh, sure, Andrew, let's look at your file."* He would yell and scream and threaten to fire him. Maybe he would fire him!

"I think about it," he said.

"Think about it!" Linda stopped and looked at Andrew. "Think about it? This isn't a time for thinking about it. This is serious. Jimmy is exploiting you. Do you know what that means?"

Linda's face was red and she was frowning.

Andrew realized that she was angry. He was embarrassed and he felt trapped. He didn't mean to make her angry. Why didn't Linda understand how he felt? Did he have to say everything out loud?

"Don't worry. I find a way to talk to Jimmy," he said. He said it to make her feel better. He didn't really think he would find a way to talk to Jimmy. It was almost impossible to talk to him even about good things.

Linda took her hand out of his. "Okay. Listen, I have a class this afternoon. We'd better go now."

Andrew wanted to ask her if she was alright. He wanted to kiss her and say that he would be just like an American and rush in and yell at Jimmy. But it wasn't true, and he didn't say anything.

CHAPTER 6

Andrew looked out the window of his apartment. He could see the backyard of the house next door. There were two fruit trees with pink blossoms on them. There was a huge tree in the corner with new, bright green leaves on it. Bunches of red tulips and yellow daffodils were planted around the edge of the lawn that was changing from its winter brown to green. But even the beautiful late-April scene wasn't enough to change Andrew's mood.

It was his day off. Since February, he had met Linda in the coffee shop every week on his day off. Not today. Linda was absent from last Thursday's class, too. He hadn't seen her or talked to her since their walk in the park a week ago. Andrew turned at the sound of Charley's bedroom door opening.

"Good morning. Are you going to work now?" Andrew asked Charley.

"Yes. I want to get there a little early. Did you hear that one of the waiters is leaving? I want to show Jimmy that I am dependable so I can get the job. What are you doing today?"

"I don't know. Maybe I'll take a walk and try to

clear my mind. It looks like a beautiful day. It reminds me of Hong Kong in a way."

"That sounds like a good way to spend your day off. Hey, how are your identity theft problems? Did you get that all cleared up?"

"Not all of it," answered Andrew, thinking about Jimmy. *"Linda helped me a lot. But I'm not sure what to do next. She gave me some advice, but I don't feel comfortable doing it her way. I need to find my own way."*

"Good luck. I have to go now. I'll see you later."

"Okay. See you later."

Andrew thought about Charley after he left. He was a nice guy and a good roommate. They weren't close friends, but they were friendly. Charley didn't bother him with lots of questions and comments about anything, not even about work, let alone the identity theft situation or YaoLin or Linda. He was easygoing and quiet. Andrew appreciated that.

Charley deserved the waiter job. Andrew wanted it less and less the more he learned about Jimmy. He hoped Charley wouldn't be hurt by Jimmy.

Andrew got a sweater and his baseball cap and went out for a walk.

Away from the busy streets, the neighborhood was calmer. He enjoyed looking at the houses and wondering who lived in them and what they did. He and YaoLin used to play a game on their walks. In his mind, he could hear her voice making up a story. *"Oh, see that swing in the backyard? These people are grandparents. Their granddaughter comes to visit once a month. The man is a retired accountant. Look at his garden. It's perfect. Now he gardens all the time. His wife is a doctor. She specializes in acupuncture. She's still working."* They could entertain themselves for hours telling stories.

Andrew sighed. He was lonely on his walk. He missed YaoLin. He never had to think about what to do when they spent time together. They always seemed to want to do the same thing. He never worried about cultural misunderstandings. Their families had known each other for many years. It wasn't like being with Linda.

That was exciting and new for him. He didn't know what to expect when he and Linda were together. She had helped him so much with his identity theft problems. Would they like each other now that there was no reason to meet? And why hadn't she called him? Maybe she would never call him again. He knew she was very disappointed in him for not wanting to confront Jimmy.

Andrew felt a chill. He looked up as he buttoned up his sweater. It was only mid-afternoon, but the sky was getting dark and the clouds were swirling around. The weather was changing. A storm was coming. He turned around and headed home.

Back in the apartment, Andrew put on some

quiet music. As he was sitting there, he realized that he completely forgot about English class that morning. He got his notebook from his backpack and sat down to write in his journal. He could go to the evening class. It would be nice to see Karen and the other students.

April 25

The storm is come too much fast. I take walk. First is sunny hot. Then is cold and wind. I so surprise see SNOW! I worry the flower's and tree's. Will all be die tomorrow? Denver all time have crazy weather in spring? I sorry I don't came class this morning. I forgot. I have too much thoughts on my brain.

After Karen talked about the day's topic with the whole class, she put the students into small groups to work together while she read journals with individual students.

"Hi, Andrew," she said. "This is a surprise to see you in the evening class. Are you going to start coming more often?"

"Maybe. I don't know. I will come in morning when I can. Is more long time than evening class."

"You're right. But you can come to both if you want. Can I see your journal?"

Karen read it quickly. Even with the mistakes,

she understood what Andrew wanted to say. Then she wrote a response.

> The storm did come very quickly. You are lucky that you took a walk today. The weather report said it will be cold with scattered flurries for the next few days. But the snow is very wet, so it melts quickly. I think the flowers and trees will be okay. At least it wasn't a blizzard like we had two years ago! There was a lot of damage to the trees then.
>
> I have a lot on my mind, too. We all lead busy lives.

"I underlined two patterns. If you have any questions about when we use the apostrophe 's' or 'too much,' you can look in the grammar book or ask me."

"Thank you, Karen. I look the book."

"Okay. You're welcome."

When he got home, Andrew decided to check his email. He knocked on Wei's bedroom door, but Wei wasn't there. Andrew knew Wei wouldn't mind if he used his computer. He logged on to his email account and saw that he had two messages. One was from Linda. One was from YaoLin. He printed them and took them into his bedroom to read them.

He read the email from Linda first. It said:

Dear Andrew,

I have been thinking a lot about our last time together in Washington Park. I'm sorry, but I can't do anything more for you concerning your identity theft situation and problems with Jimmy. You know what I think you should do, and I can't understand why you let yourself be pushed around by that man. He can cause major problems for you that will only get worse over time. At some point they will be impossible to resolve. We both know Jimmy is lying and exploiting you and the other workers, and he's probably selling your identities as well. I can't fix this for you.

I didn't come to class last week because I didn't want to see you until I was clear in my own mind. I talked to Karen and have decided to take a break from volunteering until September to focus on my art.

I enjoyed our times together. You are an amazing cook and a good dancer. Maybe we will see each other again some day. I look forward to that day in the future when we meet in the coffee shop and you tell me your identity theft story with a happy ending. Until then, I wish you all the best.

Linda

Andrew read the email three times. Each time he understood more until he felt he knew what Linda was saying. It was not a letter of apology. She was telling him goodbye. She didn't want to see him again until he solved his problem with Jimmy—until he confronted Jimmy with his lies.

Andrew sat back in his chair and closed his

eyes. It seemed like his stomach dropped to his feet. He felt completely alone in an unknown world.

Finally, he opened his eyes. He had been sitting there in a daze for a long time. As he got up, he noticed the other email that he had printed. He didn't have the energy to read it then. He took it with him to his bedroom and put it on his bedside table.

All night long, Andrew tossed and turned in bed. He worried about what Jimmy could do. Was Linda right? Did he have to confront Jimmy like Linda said, or was there another way? Would he ever see Linda again? Would he solve these problems?

At sunrise he remembered YaoLin's email. Why was she writing him? Would she be irritated with him, too? They had talked on the phone several times since her visit to Denver. They were still friends, but it was different now that they weren't engaged. Andrew rolled over to pick up the email. He read:

Dear Yingen,

With this email, I send my sincere wishes that you are well and happy. What I have to say is important. Please think about what is in your heart.

I have thought about us a lot since I returned from Denver. That trip doesn't seem real now. Everything was difficult since you had to work and I could not speak English, and it was so cold. I was not happy there.

But now that I am back home in Hong Kong, I remember what

good times we had here, and how compatible we are, and our plans to get married. I know you said you were not ready to leave the U.S. I am asking you to come back to Hong Kong for a visit, so we can see if things would be good for us again. I am now taking English classes.

I will wait for you to call or email me.

Love,

YaoLin

Andrew lay in bed, thinking. Maybe this was the answer. Maybe he should go back to Hong Kong. But when? Now? He loved YaoLin, didn't he? They were a good couple. Maybe he could forget all about learning more English and seeking new opportunities. He could get a job as a chef again and not have to be a busboy. Or, since YaoLin was learning English, maybe she would change her mind and move to the U.S.

On the other hand, could he live with himself knowing that Jimmy was still doing things that were against the law? No, he couldn't. He would have to take action. And what about Linda? What did he feel for her? Did she have feelings for him? Or was their romantic relationship over before it really got started?

CHAPTER 7

The next morning, Andrew got up and made tea. It was still early, and he wasn't hungry, so he sat at the table and sipped his tea. He decided to write his journal entry for his next English class. He looked at the journal prompt: Tell about springtime in your country.

April 26

In Hong Kong it is raining all time right now. It is hot, maybe 85 degrees Fahrenheit. If I will be there, I will not go outside too much. My girlfriend and I will plan our wedding. My mother, shes mother will be very happy. In Denver, it is raining right now. But it is cool. Flowers are coming.

Andrew stopped writing. He closed his journal and poured more tea. Wei came into the kitchen. He rubbed his eyes and yawned. He opened the refrigerator door and mumbled something.

"What?" asked Andrew.

Wei looked over the door at Andrew. "The early bird gets the worm," he said.

"What's a worm?"

Wei still spoke in English. "You know, birds eat worms. They live in the dirt."

"It's too early to speak English," said Andrew, *"Especially idioms."*

Wei raised his eyebrows. *"Sorry,"* he said. He poured himself some tea. *"What's wrong?"*

Andrew sighed. *"I got two emails yesterday. One was from Linda. She told me goodbye. She only wants to go out with me if I confront Jimmy with my suspicions about him. The other email was from YaoLin. She wants me to go back to Hong Kong. She wants me to give our relationship another chance."*

Wei nodded. *"Those are two smart women."*

Andrew looked at him, a question on his face.

Wei put a pot of water on the stove for rice soup. *"Linda is right about Jimmy,"* he explained.

"I think so, too," Andrew admitted. *"Jimmy is a bad guy. He's hurting Chinese people with his work practices."*

"And if he's an identity broker *then he's even worse than we think,"* said Wei. *"We have to stop him. Let's decide what to do."*

"You might get in trouble," said Andrew.

"Jimmy can't hurt me. My job is secure, and I have my residence card."

Andrew shook his head. *"That's not what I mean. Jimmy might do something. Something violent or destructive."*

"Have you ever seen him do anything like that?"

"Not me, but the cook told me he thought Jimmy had some of his thugs beat up one of the waiters who tried to quit because he wanted more pay."

"That makes it even more important for someone to do something."

Wei sat down at the table.

Andrew leaned on the table with his head in his hands. *"If we make a plan and Jimmy gets arrested, he'll go to jail. Then everyone at the restaurant will be out of work. No one will thank me for that."*

"That's true," said Wei. *"But I think most of them can get better jobs. I don't think all restaurant owners are like Jimmy."*

"I hope not!" said Andrew. He spooned the rice soup into two bowls, one for Wei and one for himself. He changed the subject. *"What do you think about what YaoLin said?"*

"She's right, too," said Wei.

"Do you think I should go back to Hong Kong?"

"Yes, for a visit. You know I like Linda. But I think you should marry a Chinese girl. It's too hard to marry outside your culture. You and Linda will never really understand each other. You can't speak Chinese with her. Even though your English is getting good, you can't communicate like you can with someone who speaks your mother tongue. And, with YaoLin, you won't have to explain everything. You already know so much about each other."

"But YaoLin and I don't want the same things anymore."

"Maybe she'll change her mind about the U.S. Maybe you just need time in a familiar place to remember that you're right for each other."

Andrew didn't know if he agreed with Wei. But he was grateful to Wei for speaking seriously with him and for offering him advice. He needed someone to help him think these two problems through. He was glad Wei was willing to help.

Charley came into the kitchen. *"Good morning,"* he said. He got himself a bowl of soup. He sat down at the table. *"Are you working today, Andrew?"* he asked.

Andrew smiled. *"You must be sleepy,"* he said. *"Of course I'm working. It's Wednesday."*

Charley grinned. *"I have a meeting with Jimmy this morning. That other waiter left, and my contract is up next week. I think he's going to promote me to waiter."*

Andrew congratulated Charley, but he felt even worse than he had before about this news. If he got Jimmy in trouble, Charley would lose everything.

Although the sky was still cloudy, the sun was beginning to shine as Charley and Andrew walked to work. Charley talked about the new job. He was very excited. He saw the waiter job as a stepping stone. *"Some day Jimmy will retire,"* he said. *"Then I'll be manager. Maybe one day, I'll open my own restaurant!"* The more Charley talked, the more worried Andrew became. He couldn't ruin Charley's new career. He couldn't expose Jimmy.

When they got to the restaurant, Jimmy and the cook were already there. Andrew went to help the cook. Charley went into Jimmy's small office. Jimmy closed the door. Soon, the sound of raised voices came through the closed door. It was impossible not to listen.

"You have no proof," yelled Charley. *"Just because I locked up last night doesn't mean I took money! Anyone could have taken it! I didn't cash out; I don't know who did. Who signed the cashier log?"*

"It's your signature," yelled Jimmy. *"Return the money or I'll report you to the police. You'll be on the first plane to China."*

Andrew and the cook looked at each other. Andrew was stunned. Charley would never steal money. And, especially, he would never steal money from Jimmy. He respected Jimmy.

The cook shook his head. *"I've seen this before. It happened last week with one of the waiters. Jimmy must have promised Charley more than he wants to deliver."* He reached in his pocket for a pack of cigarettes. *"I'm going outside for a smoke."*

Andrew didn't know what to do. Charley and Jimmy continued to yell at each other. Then Jimmy screamed, *"Get out of my restaurant. Don't ever come back. You're fired."*

Charley threw open the door. He looked at Andrew but didn't seem to see him. His face was red and furious. He rushed by Andrew and out of the kitchen through the alley door. Jimmy stormed after him. At the door he yelled, *"Don't try to get a job at another restaurant. I know plenty of people. I'll make sure you never work in Denver again."*

Jimmy turned back into the kitchen. Andrew felt like his feet were stuck to the floor with glue. He stared at Jimmy. He couldn't look away. Jimmy didn't even look angry. He had a little smile on his face.

"Charley quit. He didn't even give me notice. It's a good thing I have a new guy starting today. I met him in Hong Kong on my last trip." Jimmy walked through the kitchen to his office. He turned to Andrew again before he went in. *"You show the new guy Sam what to do today."*

Andrew waited until Jimmy closed his door. Then he went into the alley where the cook was finishing his cigarette.

"Where did Charley go?" he asked.

The cook threw his cigarette butt on the ground and stepped on it. As he ground it into the damp asphalt of the alley, he pointed to the street. *"That way,"* he said. *"My advice is don't get involved. I told you what happened to the waiter. Charley's not the first one."*

"I'm going to talk to Charley," said Andrew. *"I'll be back in 15 minutes."*

He didn't care if Jimmy got mad at him for leaving. He had to see Charley. He ran down the alley and turned toward the apartment. He thought he could catch up with him if he ran hard. Soon, he saw Charley, his back stiff, hurrying along the sidewalk.

"Charley!" Andrew called. *"Wait!"*

Charley turned around. His face was still red, but now he looked both angry and scared. He waited for Andrew.

"Do you know what just happened?" he asked as Andrew came near.

"I heard it all." Andrew stopped next to Charley. He was out of breath from the run.

"I don't understand what happened, Andrew. One minute I thought I was going to get a promotion. The next minute, Jimmy was telling me to get out and never come back."

The men walked together toward the apartment. It was strange to be heading back to the apartment in the cool, sunny morning rather than late at night.

"Charley, tell me again, what's the last day of your contract?" asked Andrew.

"Monday. It doesn't matter now, though. I won't get my three-year bonus or a promotion. I don't even have a job."

"What bonus?" asked Andrew.

Charley was so miserable that he didn't notice the surprise in Andrew's voice. *"The signing bonus. Jimmy said that if I signed a three-year contract with him, he would pay me a big bonus at the end."*

Jimmy didn't make that deal with Andrew. He didn't tell Charley that, but he was beginning to understand Jimmy's plan for Charley.

"So, you got promises of a signing bonus, a promotion if your English improved—"

"And, Jimmy said he would sponsor me for my residence card," said Charley.

"Those are a lot of promises," said Andrew.

"I don't know what I'll do now," said Charley.

Andrew had another thought. *"Charley, how much was Jimmy paying you?"*

"$4.00 an hour."

"That's below minimum wage!"

"I know, but he said the signing bonus would make up for it." Charley looked angry again. *"Many times, late at night when I was locking up, Jimmy told me how happy he was with my work. He told me my signing bonus would be a big one."*

Andrew remembered how Jimmy liked to stand near Charley and talk quietly to him. He always wondered what they were talking about. Now he knew. *"He never told you how much?"*

"No."

"I think I know what happened. Jimmy needed a way to get rid of you before your contract was up. He already hired someone to replace you. He accused you of stealing so that you wouldn't make any trouble about being fired. From the beginning, everything he told you and me was a big lie."

They reached the apartment. As if reflecting the men's moods, clouds swept in front of the sun. The day turned gray. Andrew shivered.

"When Wei gets home, tell him what happened. Jimmy went too far this morning. Tonight, we'll figure out what to do. We aren't going to let him get away with any more of this."

Andrew hunched his shoulders against the wind, put his hands in the pocket of his rain jacket, and headed back to the restaurant.

CHAPTER 8

Andrew went back to the restaurant. As he worked, Andrew watched Sam, the new guy, from across the room. He was small and wiry and a head shorter than Andrew. His black hair was long, and his bangs hung over his eyes. He had high cheekbones and thin lips that gave his face a mean look. He had not smiled once since he came in. Andrew showed him where everything was and what he needed to do. He was now setting the tables while Andrew filled the water pitchers.

Suddenly, a cell phone rang. It was Sam's. He took the call and spoke in Chinese for a minute. When he finished, Andrew went over to him.

"Jimmy doesn't like us to use cell phones at work, so you should probably turn that off."

"That was Jimmy calling me," answered Sam. *"I'll put it on vibrate in case he calls again."*

Andrew thought that was strange. Jimmy never called anyone else who worked at the restaurant. He wondered who Sam was. He seemed to know Jimmy pretty well.

There weren't many customers at lunch time. This was good because Jimmy hadn't replaced the waiter who left. Even though this was Sam's first meal to bus, and the restaurant wasn't busy, Sam didn't seem to care about the work. Andrew thought back to when he first started. He wanted to do his best. He hoped then that he would be promoted to waiter. Also, he knew how important every little detail was for making a good impression on the customers so they would return to the restaurant. Why was Sam so casual? There was something strange about him.

Charley was in his room with the door closed when Andrew got home. But Wei was still awake. He and Andrew sat in the living room.

"Did Charley tell you what happened today?" Andrew asked Wei.

"He said he was fired, but he didn't want to talk about it. How did he get fired? I thought he was going to get a promotion."

Andrew filled Wei in on everything. He told him about Charley's meeting with Jimmy, what the cook said, the promised signing bonus, and about Sam.

"Signing bonus! That's crazy. Who ever heard of a signing bonus for a busboy? What next?" asked Wei.

Wei encouraged Andrew to keep his eyes and ears open.

"Let's leave Charley alone tonight. But the three of us should talk this over together soon. Jimmy needs to be stopped. We'll make plans tomorrow or the day after," Wei told Andrew.

The next day, Andrew noticed how much Sam used his cell phone. He even had calls when he was in the middle of clearing a table or filling a water glass. Andrew didn't hear any ring tone, but Sam often stopped what he was doing and went to the cashier counter to speak on his phone.

That night, Andrew mentioned Sam's behavior to Wei and Charley. Charley had a blank look on his face, but Wei said, *"That makes me think of an article I read online recently. Sam could be getting credit card numbers for Jimmy."*

"How?" asked Charley and Andrew at the same time.

"His phone may have a camera in it. He can just aim it at a credit card, take a picture, and get the number. It's a big scam. People have no idea it's happening, so they don't watch out for it. Most people know about covering up the key pad when they punch in their PIN numbers at an ATM. And they take their receipts instead of throwing them away. But they don't expect anyone to take a picture of their card, especially with a cell phone camera. You can never be too careful," said Wei.

"So what should we do?" asked Charley.

"I don't think you should do anything right now. Andrew, you watch what Sam does when he is on his phone. Pay attention to the details, especially anything unusual. But be careful. Don't let anyone see what you're doing."

"I don't understand," said Andrew with a puzzled look on his face. *"Why would Jimmy have Sam take pictures of credit cards in his own restaurant? That seems stupid."*

Charley spoke. *"Maybe he was practicing. Jimmy once said something about photographing credit cards to me, but I thought he was warning me to be careful."*

"We're all tired," said Wei. *"Let's sleep on it. We'll talk again tomorrow."*

Later, lying in bed, Andrew suddenly said aloud in English, "Oh, I forget English class today again. My life is too much busy."

Maybe it was for the best. It would be difficult to concentrate on the lesson when he had so much on his mind, like Charley getting fired, Sam and cell phone cameras. He hadn't thought about his dilemmas with YaoLin and Linda for two days.

Twice during lunch Andrew noticed Sam go behind the counter and talk on his cell phone. It was a challenge to continue what he was doing and watch Sam at the same time. The first time, a couple was just leaving the cashier. The second time, a customer was at the counter paying his bill. Sam turned around toward the man and took his phone away from his ear. It happened so quickly that Andrew wasn't sure what he saw.

The restaurant was full at dinner. Andrew was too busy to watch Sam very closely. He did notice that Sam went behind the counter several times. One time he looked up to see Sam looking at him.

It was late when the staff finished cleaning up and getting the tables set for the next day. Just as Andrew put on his jacket, Jimmy came in and asked him to come to his office.

"Andrew, I'm really pleased with your work. I want to promote you to waiter. You already know what to do and you're familiar with the menu, so it should be easy for you. Can you start tomorrow?" Jimmy asked with a smile.

"I-I-I don't know," Andrew stammered in surprise.

"It will mean a raise. I'll have the papers ready for you to sign in the morning. Is it a deal?"

"I guess so."

"Good," said Jimmy. *"I'll see you tomorrow. Come in a little early."*

"Okay," said Andrew. He was so shocked, he couldn't think of anything else to say.

"That's the last thing I expected," Andrew told Wei and Charley. *"I thought maybe Sam said something and Jimmy was going to fire me, too."*

Wei had a thoughtful look on his face. *"I think Sam did talk to Jimmy. This is Jimmy's way of getting you on his side. He probably thinks that if he gives you more responsibility, you'll be tied to the restaurant and won't do anything to lose your job."*

"What do you mean?" asked Andrew.

"There's a saying in English: 'If you scratch my

back, I'll scratch yours.' *It means that if you do something for me, I'll do something for you. Jimmy's giving you a better job. In exchange, you shut your eyes and pretend nothing is happening."*

"But I can't do that! Jimmy needs to be stopped!" said Andrew.

"I agree," said Wei.

"Me, too," said Charley. *"So now what do we do?"*

"I've been thinking about this a lot," replied Wei. *"We have to get proof that Jimmy is an identity broker. That means that you, Andrew, need to look in his office and check his files. You have to find papers with names and numbers or something that will prove to the police what Jimmy is doing."*

"Okay," said Andrew. *"I'll do it. But when and how?"*

The three men talked until midnight, making plans for the next day.

Jimmy was ready with Andrew's new employment agreement. Andrew signed it. Wei, Andrew, and Charley agreed that Andrew needed to take the waiter job and try hard to do it well, or Jimmy would suspect something right away.

"Great," said Jimmy. *"I'll put this in your file. I know you'll be a good waiter. I have to go out now. But I'll be back around 5:00 this evening, so I'll see you then. Good luck."*

Andrew knew the menu, but he felt clumsy taking the orders and writing them down. The more he did it, the easier it got. He concentrated on his new duties. He couldn't watch Sam at the same time.

After lunch, Andrew chatted with the cook. Then he sat down to rest and go over his duties in his mind. Sam left with another busboy. A group of waiters and busboys was sitting at a table at the back eating lunch. The restaurant was quiet.

Andrew thought to himself, *"It's now or never."* He got up and went to Jimmy's office.

There were papers stacked on his desk and several piles on the floor. A grey file cabinet stood in the corner. Andrew tried to open the top drawer. Locked. He tried the others. All locked. He went to the desk and opened a folder on one of the piles. It was his folder. The papers he had signed just a few hours earlier were right on top.

Someone passed Jimmy's door. Andrew froze. It was only a busboy on his way to the restroom. Andrew quickly opened a few other folders. Restaurant receipts, bank statements, purchase orders but nothing that looked like a list of social security numbers or stolen identities. The busboy passed by again.

Andrew jiggled the mouse on Jimmy's computer. The screen filled with names and numbers. Andrew looked closely. They must be credit card numbers! How could he get a copy of them? Quickly, he called Wei at work. Wei answered on the first ring.

"I'm in Jimmy's office now," whispered Andrew. *"Wei, I found something on his computer. Lots of names and numbers. What should I do?"*

"Send them to me," Wei said.

Just as Andrew pressed "send," he saw a movement out of the corner of his eye. It was Sam. He was standing outside Jimmy's office door talking on his cell phone.

Andrew grabbed his folder and ran. He brushed past Sam, ran through the kitchen and out the back door of the restaurant. He didn't look back until he had crossed Broadway. He saw the cook standing outside the restaurant beside Sam and pointing in the opposite direction.

Andrew burst in the door of the apartment.

"Charley, I just called Wei at work. I found some names and numbers on Jimmy's computer and sent them to him. And I got my folder. But Sam saw me. Jimmy wasn't there, but I think he knows I was in his office because Sam was on his phone. He could come here."

"Here?" cried Charley. *"Then you have to call the police. We're in danger! Call the police! If you don't, I will."*

Andrew realized that what Charley said was true. He picked up the phone and dialed 911.

CHAPTER 9

After the 911 call to the police, Andrew and Charley waited in the apartment. Very soon there was a loud banging at the front door.

Andrew and Charley looked at each other. It seemed too soon for the police to be there.

"*Who do you think it is?*" whispered Charley.

"I'm not sure," said Andrew. Quietly he crept to the door and looked out the peephole. Jimmy and Sam were standing outside. Their faces were dark and angry. Andrew was about to move away, when Jimmy yelled, "*Open the door, you jerks!*" He threw his shoulder into the door. Andrew jumped back.

"*We have to get out,*" he whispered.

Charley motioned for Andrew to follow him. He went out on the balcony at the back of the apartment. The pounding on the front door grew louder and stronger as Andrew and Charley looked over the balcony railing. Below was a small parking lot where some tenants parked their cars. It was one story from the balcony to the ground.

"Do you think we can jump?" asked Charley.

Just then, they heard the sound of the front door giving way.

"They broke down the front door!" said Andrew. *"We don't have a chance! We'll have to jump."*

Charley swung one leg over the railing, then the other and, without a backward glance, leaped off the balcony. He landed like a cat, crouching down and moving close to the building. Andrew followed right behind. He felt a terrible pain in his ankle as he landed on the asphalt of the parking lot. He thought it must be broken.

"Go get help," he said. He rolled over next to a parked car.

Charley squatted next to him. *"I can't leave you like this. Besides, the police are on their way."*

"But they don't know that we're in danger right now!"

Charley reached into his pocket. He pulled out his cell phone. He dialed 911 again.

Things happened quickly after that. Charley and Andrew crawled behind the cars, down the alley, and out to some bushes by the street. As they were crawling, they heard sirens. Soon, there were police cars everywhere. The police spotted Andrew and Charley hiding under the bushes and rushed toward them.

"Put your hands behind your heads!" yelled an officer. The police thought that they were the intruders. Charley tried to tell them, in Chinese and English, that he and Andrew were the ones who called them.

"Stay calm," Andrew told Charley. *"Do everything they say. Be polite."*

"Shut up! Kneel down!" yelled the police officer.

Andrew and Charley followed the officer's instructions. Andrew was very glad that they both knew enough English to follow the directions. Any confusion could be cleared up later. Now, Andrew and Charley just needed to stay safe.

The apartment manager saw them kneeling on the ground and ran over to talk to the police. One policeman stayed with them while several others ran up to the apartment and around to the alley. In a few minutes, the officers led Sam and Jimmy to the police cars. The policeman guarding Andrew and Charley told them they could get up. "Sorry for the mix-up," he said. "You did the right thing by cooperating."

Andrew couldn't stand properly, and the police officer called in for an ambulance. He and Charley helped Andrew over to a car near where Jimmy and Sam were being held. Jimmy sneered at Andrew with eyes full of hate. As he was getting into the police car, Jimmy snarled at Andrew, *"I'll get you for this. I'll make you pay."*

"Officer, he threaten me," said Andrew coolly to the policeman. "He say he make me pay."

The officer put Jimmy in the police car. He wrote a few more sentences on his police report and said, "Don't worry, sir. We'll keep a watch on your place for a while. And this guy's not leaving the jail anytime soon."

Wei arrived just as Andrew was getting into the ambulance. He followed in his car to the hospital. Andrew's ankle was broken, and the doctors put it in a cast. Then, Wei, Charley, and Andrew were interviewed by police detectives. Within hours, Jimmy's restaurant was shut down. As Andrew feared, all the employees were out of work.

That evening, Wei, Charley, and Andrew sat, once again, in their living room. They were drinking tea and eating a take-out pizza. Soft, soothing music played. They were too excited to think about going to bed.

"How's your ankle feeling now?" Charley asked Andrew.

"Better since I took the pain-killer," said Andrew. *"How did you make those jumps without hurting yourself?"*

Charley grinned. *"I did gymnastics and martial arts when I was a kid. I guess my body remembered a few things."*

Wei sipped his tea. *"Jimmy is really in big trouble. There were hundreds of names, social security numbers, and credit card numbers on that list you sent me. I think the restaurant was just a cover for a huge identity theft operation."*

"Why do you think he stole my information? That was really stupid," said Andrew.

"It was 'the beginning of the end,'" Wei agreed.

Charley looked thoughtful. *"I think he put your name on the list by mistake. Maybe he was just testing a new system or something and used your information. Then, maybe he forgot to erase it and sold it with a big set of names."*

"You're probably right," said Andrew.

Wei finished the last bite of pizza, wiped his hands, and then folded them in his lap. He leaned forward. *"I have some good news for you, Charley. I talked to my boss today. I hope you don't mind, but I told him about your problem. This was before everything that happened here. I told him that you are a hard worker and in a difficult situation. I told him it would make it easier for you to go to the police if you felt secure. He agreed to help."*

Both Andrew and Charley were very surprised.

"That's good, but why?" asked Andrew.

"He's a great guy. Also, he really likes my work. He wants me to be happy here and stay at his company!"

The men laughed. Wei was certainly not modest.

"Charley, he has a job for you."

"Really?"

"Yes. The company has an executive dining room. They need a waiter. It's only part time, but you can get the waiter experience you want. Maybe he can help you with your work visa too."

"Is that possible?"

"Yes. The company hires lots of Chinese and Indian employees. Usually they hire for high-tech positions like mine, but the human resources department can work something out for you. You might have to go back to Hong Kong for a while, though."

Charley nodded. *"Wei, this is unexpected and very generous—"*

"Okay, just be the best employee they ever had," joked Wei. *"Don't thank me. They need a good worker, and you need a job. It works out well for everyone."*

Andrew was very happy for Charley. He hoped Wei was not going to offer him a job, though. He already had a plan.

The men talked and talked. They talked about Charley's new job and about what the other restaurant employees might do now. They wondered whether they would have to go to court and testify against Jimmy. Finally, Wei said, *"Well, Andrew, now are you going to visit Hong Kong? Now that you're unemployed you could go for a long visit."*

"No," said Andrew. *"I'm not going. I'm staying here and studying more English."*

"But what about YaoLin?"

"I'm going to call her tonight," said Andrew. *"She's a wonderful woman. But we're different now. I don't love her the same way that I did."*

Wei nodded. *"I'm not too surprised, but she will be unhappy to hear this."*

Andrew sighed. *"I don't want to make anyone*

unhappy. I still want to be her friend. Wei, I hope you'll continue to email her and talk to her on the phone, too. She likes you."

Wei looked pleased. *"Okay, I will."*

Charley stood up. *"All this love talk is too much for me. I'm going to bed. What a day!"*

The men said good night. Andrew called YaoLin from his bedroom, and they had a short but good talk. She said she was disappointed, but she didn't cry or seem to be heart broken. She also mentioned Wei. She said she hoped she could still be friends with him. After she hung up, Andrew smiled. Maybe YaoLin and Wei were a better match than Andrew and YaoLin. Who knew? Anything could happen.

May 2

I have very important question. I don't have job. My job gone. I will not look new job right now. I will look school. This class is wonderful class. But now, I have time. I don't spend many money I make in job for two years. I will go school and learn more, more English. I want go every day. Can you help me, please? Can you help me find English school for getting better, going to cooking school after learning English?

Andrew waited patiently while Karen read his journal entry. He hoped she understood it and that she could help him. If not, he was confident he could find the information he needed some other way. Nothing could stop him.

Karen wrote:

> Andrew, this is wonderful. I think you are ready to go to a more academic English class, and yes, I can help you find an English school. In fact, I know of a university here in Denver that offers a degree in cooking, or culinary arts, and also offers English classes to get you ready for the university. Does that sound good to you?

Andrew read what Karen wrote.

"Really? This university have both things like I want?" he asked.

"Yes, really," said Karen. "It has both things. Also, they offer scholarships to help you with tuition. I have a brochure in the file cabinet. Ask me for it after class."

"Can I ask question about journal?"

"Sure."

Andrew pointed at the word "degree." "I guess this is certificate?"

"Well, it's like a certificate. It proves you passed all your classes. We call it a degree. You can get a two-year degree, which is an associate's degree, or a four-year degree, which is a bachelor's degree."

Andrew nodded. "I heard this before. Now I understand better."

Later on, when he was walking slowly home from school, Andrew smiled to himself. He wished he could call Linda. He would tell her everything that had happened. He would say, in English, "Linda, I stepped up to the plate. And, I know what is my passion. I want to be chef in great restaurant."

He didn't think he could call her, though. First, he hadn't talked to her for a long time. Second, his ankle was in a cast, and he was walking with crutches. Third, he didn't have a job. She might think he just wanted her help again. She probably wasn't even interested in him anymore. Like YaoLin, he made her sad for a little while, but then she probably forgot about him. These thoughts weren't very cheerful. He decided to let the past go and move forward with his new plan.

CHAPTER 10

"Please, you have information about get degree in culinary arts?" Andrew asked the woman at the information desk of the university that Karen suggested.

"Yes. You need to go to the Registrar's office. It's down this hall, room 127." She pointed to her right and smiled.

The Registrar's office was busy. There were several lines of people waiting to speak to the school officials behind the counter. Andrew stood in the shortest line. After 20 minutes, it was his turn.

"Please, I want get degree in culinary arts."

A young man with a university ID hanging around his neck asked, "Have you filled out the registration papers yet?"

"No. I just come today, first time."

"Okay. Here are the forms you need to fill out. You can take them with you, but the last day of registration for the summer session is Friday. Do you have your documents and English certificate?"

"I have passport and certificate from my English teacher that I take class. Is enough?"

"The passport is fine. Can I see the certificate?"

Andrew handed it to the young man, who looked at it and said, "I'm not sure this is the correct document, but they can tell you in the English Center. Go there first. Someone there will check it out and help you fill out all the forms. They have counselors who can advise you on your schedule and get you set up in English classes if you need them."

"Oh, I need," said Andrew with a laugh. "Also, they tell me about scholarship?"

"Yes, they will be able to help you with everything. Here, take this catalog. You can look it over while you wait. I hope you have a few hours. Every office is pretty crowded this week."

"Many people, yes. Thank you for assistance."

In the English Center, a number of foreign students were at a big table filling out forms. Others were sitting in chairs near the receptionist's desk. Andrew heard several different languages—Spanish, Korean, and what he thought was Arabic, but not Chinese.

The receptionist told him that all the advisors were busy helping other students, so Andrew put his name on a list. There were four names ahead of his. He sat at the table and began writing the necessary information on the registration form.

A little after 6:00 PM, Andrew got off the bus and walked to his apartment. He was in a good mood.

"Did you get registered?" Wei asked him.

"Yes. I was there all day. I met with a Chinese-

American woman who is my advisor. She reminds me of my mother. She has pictures of her children and grandchildren in her office. Her parents came from Canton. She understands Chinese, but she doesn't speak it. She helped me with my schedule."

"What classes are you taking?"

"Just English for the summer. It's an intensive program, five days a week. I'm taking a conversation class and a reading and writing class. My advisor says if I do well, I can enroll in culinary classes in the fall."

"That's great. Too bad you can't continue your other English class."

"I'll miss it, but Karen was the one who told me about the university. She said her program is for general communication and life skills, not academic preparation. It's okay. Now I'm starting a new chapter in my life."

"I brought home the newspaper today," said Wei. *"There's another article about Jimmy and the identity theft ring. It says 11 more people went to the police with complaints about Jimmy. He mistreated and misled them when they were working in his restaurant, like Charley. They were all too scared to tell officials before now. By the way, how are you going to pay for school with no job?"*

Andrew answered, *"My advisor gave me a scholarship application. She thinks I have a good chance to get a lot of my classes paid for. I told her my situation and why I'm not working now. She read the story about it all in the newspaper last week. She even called me a hero."*

"Wow, should I bow to you now?" asked Wei as he bent forward from his waist.

Just then, Charley came in with a big smile on his face.

"Why are you smiling?" asked Andrew.

"I'm so glad that I don't work for Jimmy anymore! And I really like my new job. Your boss complimented me today, Wei."

"Hey, when my boss is happy, I'm happy."

June and July were hot and dry. The temperature was in the 80s or 90s most days. There was little rain. Andrew was glad the classrooms were air conditioned, but sometimes it was too cold inside. Then he joined his classmates outside under one of the big shade trees on campus. He was getting to know the other students. Several of them went to a Colorado Rockies professional baseball game and watched fireworks on the 4th of July. Andrew went to the mountains for a hike with three other men, two from Japan and one from Korea, and the girlfriend of one of them. She was small, with long black hair. He thought of YaoLin. He wondered how she was.

Coincidentally, there was a letter on the table

in her familiar handwriting when he got home. He reached for it, but it was addressed to Wei. He felt a catch in his throat.

"Oh, sorry. I meant to put that away."

"It's okay," answered Andrew. *"I thought about her today. How is she doing?"*

"Good. We've written emails to each other since May. This is the first letter she wrote. I'm thinking of going to Hong Kong to visit in September."

"September in Hong Kong. That's a great time to go there." Andrew didn't want to think about Wei and YaoLin together. He changed the subject. *"Hey, do you want to go out for dinner? We can try that Mexican restaurant on the corner."*

❖

School was difficult, but Andrew knew he was making progress. People seldom asked him to repeat what he said, so he knew he was being understood. He spent a lot of time on his lessons and homework, and it was paying off.

When the summer session was over, he had time to think of other things. He felt peaceful now when he thought of YaoLin and Wei. He was happy for them, not jealous. They were a good match.

Every day on the bus to and from school, Andrew passed the Botanic Gardens. It was beautiful from the street, with lush plants and colorful

flowers in front and framed by the distant Rocky Mountains. He imagined it was even more beautiful inside.

One afternoon in August, he decided to visit the Botanic Gardens. He went alone and wandered all around, through the rose garden and the alpine and plains areas. He lingered in the Japanese garden, enjoying the serenity of the tall willows, the smaller, sculpted trees, and the pond with the big goldfish swimming lazily around. Just sitting there resting, he felt relaxed and happy.

On his way out, Andrew noticed a sign in front of the building near the entrance. It said, "Art Show Inside Today."

He went in and wandered around. Many artists had entered their work. There were sculptures and weavings and paintings in watercolor and oil. Some were realistic, especially of flowers and nature scenes. Others were more abstract. He stopped in front of one painting that he particularly liked because of the colors and movement. He gazed at it a long time, until he was almost lost in it.

A woman came up behind him. "What do you think about my painting?" she asked. Andrew turned to talk to her. It was Linda.

"This painting speak to my head and my heart with many joy. I think I could love the woman who paint this picture."

Andrew's Recipe for Braised Fish in Soy Sauce

Four Servings
You will need a big frying pan or a Chinese wok.

Ingredients A
4 filets of firm, white fish
1 tablespoon cooking wine
1 tablespoon soy sauce
Directions
Marinate fish in wine and soy sauce.

Ingredients B
2 slices fresh ginger root
1 chopped green onion
3 tablespoons cooking oil
Directions
Heat cooking oil in a wok. Add the green onion and ginger. Add the fish and fry until it is golden.

Ingredients C
3 tablespoons soy sauce
2 tablespoons cooking wine
½ teaspoon salt
Directions
Add Ingredients C to the fish in the wok. Simmer for about 30 minutes.
Eat with rice.

Enjoy!